SCENES
FOR
TEENAGERS

Roger Karshner

SCENES FOR TEENAGERS

Scenes for young men and women of ideal duration, presented in readable type, spacing and punctuation. Slices of real life written in modern language that are perfect for auditions, readings, and class work.

If you find "Scenes For Teenagers" to you liking we recommend two other Dramaline publications: "Monologues For Teenagers" and "High School Monologues They Haven't Heard."

For information write: Dramaline Publications, 10470 Riverside Drive, Suite #201, Toluca Lake, CA 91602. 818/985-9148.

CONTENTS

GIRL/GIRL

Comments on Acting

Acting is a question of absorbing other people's personalities and adding some of your own experience.—Paul Newman.

The only thing you owe the public is a good performance.—Humphrey Bogart.

You spend all your life trying to do something they put people in asylums for.—Jane Fonda.

The main problem of the actor is not to let the audience go to sleep, then wake up and go home feeling they've wasted their money.—Laurence Oliver.

Talk low, talk slow, and don't say too much.—John Wayne.

Pray to God and say the lines.—Bette Davis.

Never work with animals of children.—Anonymous.

Tragedy is if I cut my finger. Comedy is if I walk into an open sewer and die.—Mel Brooks.

MINDY & ALBERTA

The girls debate the issue of cats versus dogs.

MINDY: Dogs are much cooler than cats.
ALBERTA: Huh uh, no way. Cats are cooler because cats are quiet and take care of themselves and don't go 'round dumping on your rug.
MINDY: But dogs are more loyal and like better friends and they can also save you if some strange dude breaks into your house late at night and tries to rob you or something or worse.
ALBERTA: Dogs are out of it. They're always running around chewing up everything and trashing the house and leaving a doggie smell in the furniture.
MINDY: Maybe, but you can have fun with 'em and they'll chase after stuff and play games and everything.
ALBERTA: Cats are too hip for that. You don't see them going around chasing after balls and sticks and junk. They're more noble and independent and don't make noise and bark and growl.
MINDY: Not my dog; not Ed, he doesn't do that. He's a good guy who always runs up to you when you come home and makes you feel welcome. Cats don't do that. They don't get off on people.
ALBERTA: Not true.
MINDY: They only come around when they want to be fed or petted or something and then they split.
ALBERTA: How about dogs? They beg around and make fools of themselves and wolf down their

food and then lie around sleeping having like these weird doggie dreams.

MINDY: Who says they dream?

ALBERTA: All you have to do is look at them. After they overeat, they lie on their back with this dopey smile on them and twitch. They're dreaming.

MINDY: No way!

ALBERTA: — of pork chops, probably. Dogs are dopes. Dummies. But not cats. They never overeat. They always check out their food first, sniff it over real good to be sure it's okay. Then they eat nice and mannerly without making a bunch of noise and leave some food in their bowl for snacks later. Smart.

MINDY: Well, you can have 'em. They're way too sneaky.

ALBERTA: Huh uh — just quiet.

MINDY: Sneaky. They slink around and poke their nose into everything. And if you don't have them declawed they'll trash your house. You should see what they did to my aunt's drapes. Like shredded.

ALBERTA: Our cats are well-behaved. Besides, they're outside cats. They stay outside and sleep out all night and do their business outside.

MINDY: So? So does Ed.

ALBERTA: Yeah, I've seen your back yard. You can't even walk across it. Yuck! And cat's cover up their business up, too.

MINDY: Which is worse because you don't know where it is and walking across your yard is like crossing a field full of land mines. Or they go in the house someplace where you can't find it and after awhile the place starts to smell like an armpit.

ALBERTA: Well, at least cats don't jump on you and slobber on your clothes.

MINDY: No. They only suck the breath out of babies.

ALBERTA: C'mon. You don't actually believe that, do you?

MINDY: That's what they say.

ALBERTA: Yeah, your stupid cat haters.

MINDY: It's a known fact.

ALBERTA: It is not.

MINDY: It is too.

ALBERTA: It isn't.

MINDY: It is.

ALBERTA: Is!

MINDY: Isn't!

ALBERTA: No way! It's an old wives' tale.

MINDY: Maybe, but I'll take my dog over your cat any day.

ALBERTA: That's because you're a cat hater.

MINDY: I am not!

ALBERTA: You are too! The last time you were over you treated the cats bad.

MINDY: You're out of it. Spaced.

ALBERTA: You ignored them. How you think that made 'em feel?

MINDY: C'mon.

ALBERTA: You hurt their feelings.

MINDY: You mean — I hurt their felix.

ALBERTA: That isn't funny!

MINDY: Okay, okay — calm down. I'm sorry, okay? Jeez!

ALBERTA: How would you like it if I snubbed your dog?

MINDY: I wouldn't. But you wouldn't snub him in the first place because he wouldn't give you a chance. He'd come up to you and be real friendly and make you feel welcome instead of slinking off and pooping behind the door.

ALBERTA: I give up!

Films are much more my level. On stage I never felt quite enough... Julie Andrews (Julia Wells).

MARTHA & BETH

Ditching school sounds a good idea. But is it?

MARTHA: I don't know. What if we get caught?
BETH: How? Who would know? So lets ditch and go hit the mall and like mess around and pig out on munchies like we planned.
MARTHA: Somebody'll see us for sure.
BETH: No chance.
MARTHA: Some geek'll see us and go back and snitch and then we're in deep trouble.
BETH: C'mon, it'll be neat. At least once.
MARTHA: What if our folks ever found out?
BETH: Nobody's going to see us.
MARTHA: It's a small world.
BETH: "It's a small world." Already you're starting to sound like an old person. Hey, Alice Miller ditches all the time.
MARTHA: So?
BETH: She's never been caught.
MARTHA: Anyway, what are we going to do all day at the mall during the middle of the week? It won't be any fun not seeing the other kids like on Saturdays.
BETH: It'll be neater. This way we'll have the whole place to ourselves for a change. Like if we wanna check out the clothes they're won't be a bunch of other people trying them on and hogging up the dressing rooms.
MARTHA: I'm tired of trying on clothes.

BETH: Then we can go to the Sleep Shop and lie around on the mattresses.

MARTHA: I don't think so.

BETH: Yesterday you were all for it.

MARTHA: Yesterday I didn't think about getting caught.

BETH: Thanks a lot, flake. Well, I'm going. You can do what you want. (*She begins to walk.*)

MARTHA: Wait a minute.

BETH: (*She holds up.*) Well, you coming or not?

MARTHA: Yes. I guess. I don't know.

BETH: (*Resumes walking.*) Forget it. I'm outta here.

MARTHA: (*Grabbing Beth's arm.*) Hold on! Relax a minute. Gimme a break. I'm trying to make up my mind.

BETH: Well … ?

MARTHA: Okay. All right, I'll go.

BETH: Great.

MARTHA: But we have to be careful, okay? I mean like check out the mall real good for people we know and everything.

BETH: Sure, sure.

MARTHA: Maybe we should just hang out in furniture stores and appliance places and like that and stay away from the clothing shops. Just to be on the safe side.

BETH: Are you kidding? I'm gonna check out some styles.

MARTHA: People are going to be watching us.

BETH: What people?

MARTHA: Sales people.

BETH: So what? What can sales people do?

MARTHA: Stare.

BETH: Huh?

MARTHA: Stare at us and make us feel guilty because they'll know that we should be in school. Old people can make you feel crummy by just looking at you.

BETH: Who cares?

MARTHA: I'm starting to worry about you.

BETH: Worry about me?

MARTHA: About your attitude. About not caring about what people think when you know you're doing something wrong.

BETH: Hey, look! Are we going to stand around here arguing all day or are we going to hit the mall like we planned?

MARTHA: I'm not going.

BETH: Okay by me. You go on to school and sit through Old Man Berg showing films about ancient Egypt. While you're looking at dumb pictures, I'll be checking out cute shoes.

MARTHA: Oh wow! I forgot all about Old Man Berg. What a dork. And his breath is awful.

BETH: Yeah, and today he's going to cover the "exciting" subject of the pharaohs. No way. Forget it. While he's covering the pharaohs, I'll be covering sportswear.

MARTHA: Both of us are going to be covering sportswear. Let's do it!

(*They exit quickly arm in arm.*)

EDNA & JOYCE

Edna, emotionally damaged by child molestation, finds it difficult speaking of her father's indiscretions. Joyce, who was similarly violated when young, has healed because she has opened up regarding her feelings. Here she encourages Edna to express her feelings and experience relief through catharsis.

EDNA: It's just — just — I can't talk about it.

JOYCE: You have to.

EDNA: I can't.

JOYCE: You've got to get it out in the open —

EDNA: No.

JOYCE: — and deal with it.

EDNA: I've tried.

JOYCE: Or you'll never get any better.

EDNA: I can't, I told you!

JOYCE: It wasn't easy for me either. For anybody whose been through it.

EDNA: It's private.

JOYCE: It's not like you're going to tell the whole world here.

EDNA: Sometimes I feel like the whole world already knows.

JOYCE: Because you feel bad about yourself because things like that don't happen to nice people, right?

EDNA: Yeah, right. Like that.

JOYCE: You feel like this big piece of garbage inside because of it —

EDNA: Please!

JOYCE: — because what your father did.

EDNA: Stop it!

JOYCE: Talk about it —

EDNA: No.

JOYCE: — all of it. Get it out.

EDNA: Leave me alone.

JOYCE: OPEN UP DAMMIT!

(Edna is shocked by this and there is a long pause.)

EDNA: *(Slowly, hesitatingly.)* It — it started when, when I was just six.

JOYCE: Yeah?

EDNA: Just six years old.

(Pause.)

JOYCE: What started?

EDNA: The stuff, you know? The stuff with my dad.

JOYCE: His molesting you.

EDNA: Yes.

JOYCE: Tell me about it.

(Pause.)

EDNA: He'd, he'd come to my room at night and wake me up. Then he'd, then he'd —

JOYCE: He'd what? What?

EDNA: — put his hand under the covers and —

JOYCE: Yes?

EDNA: — touch me. It was awful.

JOYCE: Of course, sure it was. Then what?

EDNA: I don't know.

JOYCE: Sure you do. C'mon.

(Pause.)

EDNA: As time went on he got bolder. He'd pull back my covers and then he'd take off my nightgown and stand me up in bed. And then he'd take off his clothes and make me — force me to touch him. *(Finding it difficult to continue.)* And he'd make me do things to him. He'd never say anything; he'd just take my hands and guide them. And then he'd touch me. And touch me and TOUCH ME! *(Breaking.)* My father, my own father. Making me do these things that scared me and made me cry. And when I'd cry he'd put his hand over my mouth and I would feel like I was drowning in fear. The bastard! The unfeeling, unloving, dirty bastard! I loved him. My father. Bastard! Bastard! *(Lapses into a sobbing.)*

JOYCE: *(Taking her in her arms.)* It's okay, it's okay. *(Pause.)* You're right, you know, he *was* a bastard. That's exactly what he was. Mine too. All of them are, molesters. Here you are this vulnerable little kid and someone you love and trust comes along and takes advantage of you and confuses you and shoots your security to hell and gives you scars you carry around inside forever. It turns you around and loads you with guilt and makes you feel like dirt —

EDNA: Yes.

JOYCE: — like crap.

EDNA: Like you're crap.

JOYCE: But you're not crap. *We're* not! No way. Remember that. Remember who's to blame here. Hey! We're the victims? Remember that, okay?

EDNA: Okay.

KATHRYN & SALLY

Kathryn carries deep-seated resentment for her father who has recently returned to his wife and family after a period living with a younger woman. In this confrontation, Sally, Kathryn's older sister, argues for understanding and forgiveness now that their father has returned to the household.

KATHRYN: Get lost!

SALLY: No.

KATHRYN: Lemme alone.

SALLY: Don't be so self-centered.

KATHRYN: I'm not.

SALLY: Like hell.

KATHRYN: I'm not having anything to do with him.

SALLY: You're out of it.

KATHRYN: Why should I?

SALLY: Because he's your father.

KATHRYN: So what?

SALLY: So you have to show him some caring.

KATHRYN: Like he showed us? Like he showed mother when he decided to walk?

SALLY: That's past.

KATHRYN: But I'm not forgetting. Walking out on Mom after all those years for some young slut.

SALLY: But he came back.

KATHRYN: Too late. You just don't come waltzing into the house again like you've been away for the weekend and say, "Hi," and expect everything to be wonderful...the same.

SALLY: He deserves a second chance.

KATHRYN: He would have never come back if Mom wasn't dying.

SALLY: He didn't know that. He never knew. He came back because he'd made a mistake and because he still loved her.

KATHRYN: He came back because he was guilty.

SALLY: ~~Jesus~~! *Oh for Pete's sake!*

KATHRYN: That's the only reason. He can say what he wants. I don't believe him.

SALLY: Your attitude sucks.

KATHRYN: You saw how she was after he ran off with that bitch. You saw her and how much she was hurt and how it ran her down.

SALLY: But that doesn't mean anything now.

KATHRYN: She loved him and trusted him more than anything and he goes and dumps on her for some young ~~whore~~. *pig.*

SALLY: So he blew it, okay?

KATHRYN: All those years she gave him. Don't they count for something?

SALLY: Of course.

KATHRYN: He could have tried to work it out instead of making it with that slut.

SALLY: Be fair. You don't know anything about her.

KATHRYN: She was a young slut who had the hots for an older man and didn't give a damn about his wife or family. She was a ~~bitch~~ *slut* and he was a fool!

SALLY: Right now you're being the fool.

KATHRYN: Go to hell!

SALLY: Easy.

KATHRYN: ~~Screw~~ *Buzz* off!
SALLY: Easy, I said!
KATHRYN: ~~Screw off!~~
SALLY: *(She grabs Kathryn and shakes her convincingly.)* SHUT UP! *(Pause.)* Now look. Just who do you think you are sitting around in judgement of people and a situation you don't know anything about, not really. Right now, if you had any feelings, any caring, you'd be reaching out to Dad at a time he needs you most of all. You've seen him, how he looks and acts and how guilty he is and how much he's shattered by Mom's illness. What he needs now is our love and understanding, not a load dumped on him about the past. So get it together, okay? Grow up and realize what you've got here and what's going down and how much is at stake. Okay? Because if you don't, if you don't drop the hatred, you're going to regret it someday when you're older and need a father and need to feel connected. Right now Dad needs our love. Okay, so he was wrong. So get over it! And another thing — the next time you tell me to screw off, get ready to drop.

What I learned from Mr. Bogart I learned from a master, and that, God knows, has stood me in very good stead. Lauren Bacall (Betty Jean Perske).

KIM & JANET

Kim and Janet have just been involved in an auto accident. Here they assess the damage and discuss parental ramifications.

KIM: Wow! Jeez. Look at it.

JANET: Trashed.

KIM: I ~~didn't even~~ hardly ∧even hit him.

JANET: Totally trashed.

KIM: Dad'll go crazy. He'll freak.

JANET: Check out the grill. Wow.

KIM: I'll be grounded for six months.

JANET: C'mon.

KIM: You don't know how he gets when he gets mad. He gets this crazy Rambo look in his eyes. He got mad once while fixing breakfast and squeezed up a bunch of waffles.

JANET: Wow.

KIM: What am I gonna do, Janet?

JANET: You just walk in and tell 'im what happened, that's what.

KIM: "You just walk and and tell 'im what happened, that's what." Are you kidding? You just don't walk in and tell you dad about stuff like this. It's not healthy. Besides, how would it sound? "Gee, Dad, this kinda bad thing happened today. Like I was driving along changing a cassette and not watching where I was going and I ran into this guy. The car's trashed but, what the heck, we've got insurance."

JANET: The main thing is, you're not hurt. Look on the bright side.

KIM: There is no bright side. In fact, a nice clean fracture might help. That way I might get sympathy. *(Surveying the damage.)* Just look at it, Janet, have you ever seen such a mess in your life?

JANET: You aren't going to tell him about the cassette changing bit are you?

KIM: It's the truth.

JANET: Hey! this is no time for the truth. Look, you tell 'im there was this little old lady who stepped off the curb without warning and you swerved to miss her and smacked the other car.

KIM: *(Thinking.)* Not bad.

JANET: You can't admit to being a screw-up.

KIM: If I was lucky I'd been killed.

JANET: C'mon on, get real.

KIM: I'm dead meat anyhow, soon as Dad sees this. A mess. A brand new car.

JANET: It looks like it got real old and wrinkled alluva sudden.

KIM: And then — the insurance. You're looking at big bucks here, Janet. The premium will skyrocket. And Dad lives in constant fear of that. He's always talking about it; how the insurance companies are looking for excuses to raise your rates. He's got this real thing about it. Damn — the very first time I drive it, too.

JANET: You think maybe it's totaled?

KIM: Don't say that, don't even think it.

JANET: It doesn't take much these days. A little smack anymore and they send 'em to the crusher where they squeeze 'em up into little steel cubes —

KIM: Please.

JANET: — and the insurance guys only pay off on only a fraction of the car's actual value.

KIM: Stop it!

JANET: Okay, okay.

KIM: What are we going to do?

JANET: We?

KIM: You have to help me.

JANET: I'll come on home with you.

KIM: Good idea.

JANET: *(After a pause.)* What time does your dad get home?

KIM: Oh, about six. How come?

JANET: Great. This way we get to show it to your mom first. Like she'll be real upset but not unreasonable like your dad and she'll understand and be relieved you're not hamburger and she'll come up with something for your old man. We'll give her the little old lady story.

KIM: Great idea.

JANET: Moms are cool when things get crazy.

KIM: Yeah. She'll soften him up. She's real good at that.

JANET: Remember, the little old lady, okay? Like real feeble with this tattered shawl and a cane and everything.

KIM: Let's not get carried away here, okay?

JANET: Maybe you should throw in that she was leading this little old, pitiful, mangy dog, too.

KIM: Janet, now I know why you get As in creative writing.

18

✓ ANGELA & MARY

Angela attempts to console Mary whose long-term, steady relationship has just ended.

ANGELA: Tough, isn't it?

MARY: I'm dying.

ANGELA: But you'll get over it.

MARY: Easy for you to say.

ANGELA: In a couple of months you won't know Roger ever existed.

MARY: I don't know.

ANGELA: I felt the same way when Dave and I broke up. I was a mess; running around in a daze, feeling sick inside, spaced.

MARY: Like you want to puke.

ANGELA: Yeah.

MARY: It's awful.

ANGELA: It'll pass.

MARY: We've been going steady for almost two years, know that?

ANGELA: Two years is too long, anyhow.

MARY: I've never been so depressed. I feel like crying all the time.

ANGELA: So go ahead and cry. Crying's no sin, you know. What happened to you guys, anyway?

MARY: It's that new girl. The tall skinny one who just moved here from Canada.

ANGELA: Darla King.

MARY: The bitch. The skinny little bitch! I'll bet she puts on that French accent. I'll bet on it.

ANGELA: You're cuter than her anytime. Ever see her legs? They're the worst. Bigger at the bottoms than at the tops. They look like they're on upside down.

MARY: Little bitch. She started out dating Corky, Roger's friend. Then they break up, okay? Then, right after, Roger starts making up these excuses why he can't see me so much. Stuff like us being together so much is messing up his grades. Then he starts copping out on weekends and when I call him it's like I'm talking into a dead phone.

ANGELA: Dave did that. Same thing. Got real indifferent.

MARY: Then Corky tips me off that Roger's seeing Darla King on the side.

ANGELA: Dave was messing around too. I caught him. I showed up at his house unexpectedly one afternoon and caught him with his hand on some girl's boob. Creep. And she had nothing — pancakes.

MARY: It's like I've got this heart ache all over.

ANGELA: Well, it's better to ache now and know the truth than go on being lied to.

MARY: I guess so.

ANGELA: You don't need people dumping on you.

MARY: No.

ANGELA: You'll get over it and be better off and meet someone nicer. Like I did Ernie. Ernie's ten times neater than Dave.

MARY: Nobody's cooler than Roger.

ANGELA: Even that new guy from California?

MARY: Nobody.

ANGELA: He's a dream, are you kidding?

MARY: He's okay, I guess. If you like the type.

ANGELA: And guess what? Don't look now, but here he comes.

MARY: What?

ANGELA: And is he ever *beautiful.*

MARY: *(She begins to primp with a frenzy.)* Oh no! Not the way I look.

ANGELA: Here he comes. Now just relax and smile. Forget about Roger.

MARY: *(Primping.)* Roger who?

You have to be a little unreal to be in this business.
Kim Basinger.

"Gone With the Wind"
Some Background and Reviews

The movie was released in 1939 by MGM. Produced by David O. Selznick. It was adapted from Margret Mitchell's novel by Sidney Howard and others. There were three directors—Victor Flemming, George Cukor, and Sam Wood. The assistant director was Lyle Wheeler. Photography was by Ernest Haller and Ray Rennahan. The musical score was by Max Steiner. The production designer was William Cameron Menzies. The editors were Hal C. Kern and James E. Newton.

A major event in the history of the industry but only a minor event in the motion picture art. There are moments when the two categories meet on good terms, but the long stretches between are filled with mere spectacular efficiency. — Franz Hoellering, The Nation.

Perhaps the key plantation movie. — Time Out.

Forget it, Louis, no Civil War picture ever made a nickle.—Irving Thalberg to Louis B. Mayer, 1936.

BOY/BOY

"Citizen Kane"
Some Background and Reviews

Released in 1941 by RKO. Produced and directed by Orson Wells. Written by Herman J. Mankiewicz and Orson Wells. Photographed by Gregg Toland. Music by Bernard Herrmann. Art director Van Nest Polglase. Special effects by Vernon L. Walker.

On seeing it for the first time, one got a conviction that if the cinema could do that, it could do anything.—Penelope Houston.

Probably the most exciting film that has come out of Hollywood for twenty-five years.—C. A. Lejeune.

More fun that any great movie I can think of.—Pauline Kael.

DONNY & HARRY

Teen alcoholics discuss their problem.

DONNY: *(Taking a seat next to Harry.)* Hi.
HARRY: Hi.
   (Pause.)
DONNY: How ya doin'?
HARRY: Okay.
   (Pause.)
DONNY: I haven't seen you here before.
HARRY: Huh uh.
DONNY: First time?
HARRY: Yeah.
DONNY: I've been in the program a year.
HARRY: A year?
DONNY: I've been clean for over nine months.
HARRY: Nine months, huh? Wow.
DONNY: Yeah. *(A Pause, then he extends his hand.)* My name's Donny.
HARRY: *(Shaking.)* Harry.
DONNY: Good t' know ya.
HARRY: Nine months, huh?
DONNY: Yeah. And it feels good, man.
HARRY: I hope I can make it.
DONNY: You can. You can do it.
HARRY: You think?
DONNY: What other choice do you have? You can't go through life messed up. It isn't living.
HARRY: I've only been off a day. Already it's a hard thing.

DONNY: For everyone in the room, man. All these people feel just like you.

HARRY: You think?

DONNY: Sure. The same. *(An all encompassing gesture.)* This is it. You have friends here. These people have all been through it. You're not alone. Not any more. Everybody in here is pulling for everybody else.

HARRY: That's good.

DONNY: How'd you get hooked?

HARRY: At home. We had stuff around the house. Hard stuff. Me and another guy usta get into it. Only difference is, he never got strung-out like me.

DONNY: It happens, man, it happens.

HARRY: He doesn't speak to me now.

DONNY: Like I said, it happens.

HARRY: An' my mom's a juicer. She's in AA now, too. She talked me into it, into trying out the program.

DONNY: With me it started in when I was playing bass with this group. Started with beer. Like at first just a couple brews a night, understand? Then three, then four, until.... Before you know it I'm getting smashed every night. Then I started hitting it during the day. I was buzzed most a the time in school.

HARRY: Me too. The stuff got hold of me. Now my life's garbage. There are whole days I can't account for. Whole days.

DONNY: I was getting bombed and doing off-the-wall stuff. I was busted twice for drunk driving. My life was screwed. I was on the way down, man.

I was dying and didn't even know it. Then this guy, our keyboard player, ups and hits the wall.
HARRY: Died?
DONNY: Just like that. Doing booze, doing blow, doing crack, doing smack, doing everything.
HARRY: Wow. Damn.
DONNY: It scared me real bad. Got me to thinking. I asked for help. This dude I was doing part time work for set me up with this rehab place down near San Diego and I got myself together and then got into the program and now I'm straight.
HARRY: What makes it even harder is living with the old lady and watching her staring at the walls and moaning like some animal 'cause she wants a drink so bad she can die. And I know what's she's going through 'cause most of the time I feel the same way; feel like I'm going to bug out. It's like your will power's in this straight jacket trying to bust loose, ya know?
DONNY: Look around. Everyone in here knows where you're coming from, okay? That's what's so cool about it. You can lean on these people. There's strength and understanding here. Like you can lean on me, too, if you want. I'll help you make it. We can help each other, understand?
HARRY: But I've only been clean for a day, man.
DONNY: So, so what? Like they say — one day at a time.

COLIN & ERNIE

It's not easy being the new kid on the block.

COLIN: The kids here are jerks.
ERNIE: C'mon.
COLIN: Jerks.
ERNIE: They don't mean to be. I mean, it's just that they're involved with their own stuff, that's all.
COLIN: This gives them the right to be jerks?
ERNIE: It's human nature. They'll come around eventually.
COLIN: And in the mean time I don't count. It's like I don't exist here or something because I'm new. I've never seen such a bunch of stuck up jerks.
ERNIE: Hey! I came up to you, didn't I?
COLIN: Yes, but —
ERNIE: — and introduced myself and started talking.
COLIN: One person. Big deal.
ERNIE: It's a lot more than you did.
COLIN: Get off my back.
ERNIE: Maybe you're like the snob around here.
COLIN: Get lost.
ERNIE: I'm just giving you some of the crap you've been dishing out, that's all, some off the bullshit that you've been —
COLIN: Okay okay, I get the point. *(Pause.)* But I still say they could be more friendly to a new kid.
ERNIE: You're going to have to meet people half way. Maybe it's your problem.

COLIN: You don't know squat about me. You talk to me five minutes and already you're making judgements.
ERNIE: Hey, man, relax, okay?
(Pause.)
COLIN: It's not easy for me. Just walking up to people, that is. It's hard for me.
ERNIE: I used to be the same way. I'd hang back, just like you. But my dad gets transferred so often and we bounce all over the place so much that I finally realized if I was ever going to have friends I'd have to make an effort.
COLIN: They're still jerks.
ERNIE: You have a rotten attitude.
COLIN: I just don't appreciate being treated like I'm from outer space, that's all. Back home the kids were friendly. But here they look at me like I'm some kinda freak, or something.
ERNIE: It's the same deal everywhere. Even back at your old school. The same. What about you?
COLIN: Huh?
ERNIE: How'd you used to treat new guys coming into your school?
COLIN: I don't remember.
ERNIE: Sure you do. You ignored them, just like they're ignoring you here.
COLIN: I don't remember.
ERNIE: Hey, you had plenty of new kids being transferred in all the time and most of them were feeling just like you: lost and lonely and scared ~~and pissed~~ because alluva sudden their life had been

turned upside down. And they hated your guts and thought you were a jerk because you didn't give a good crap about 'em.

COLIN: Are you calling me a jerk?

ERNIE: That's what *you're* calling everybody.

COLIN: That's different.

ERNIE: The same thing, face it! You're going to have to give 'em a break, okay? In time they'll come around and stuff will work out. But in the meantime, you're going to have to open up. So you get rejected. Big deal. So what? You're going have to take a shot. Like I did with you. I walked up to you cold, didn't I?

COLIN: Maybe you shouldn't have.

ERNIE: Maybe you're right. 'Cause all I've been hearing is complaints and about how everything is the pits and how everybody is a jerk. Well, you know what they say about jerks.

COLIN: What?

ERNIE: It takes one to know one.

I'll always be there because I'm a skilled professional. Whether or not I have any talent is beside the point. Michael Caine (Maurice Micklewhite).

DAVID & CLARK

The guys bemoan the curse of acne.

DAVID: *(Checking out his face in a mirror.)* A mess.

CLARK: Yeah. Tell me about it.

DAVID: A rotten mess. My face has more bumps than a stucco wall.

CLARK: Worse.

DAVID: Hey! Look who's talking!

CLARK: I'm just being realistic, that's all.

DAVID: *(Noting his face.)* Damn.

CLARK: You ever think we'll out grow it?

DAVID: If we don't, we'll never make out.

CLARK: Ooh! What a depressing thought.

DAVID: If you were a girl would you wanna be seen with a guy with a face like a veal cutlet?

CLARK: I've tried everything. Nothing works. They start out this little red bump and wind up an egg yolk.

DAVID: Gross. You're making me sick.

CLARK: I guess it's just nature.

DAVID: It's fast food. It's loaded with fat. Like eating moulded grease. And it goes right to zits. A Big Mac and fries is worth about ten, I figure.

CLARK: I still say it's nature. Damn. I'm sick of my face looking like a car wreck.

DAVID: At least we're not alone. Half the guys in school are pussed-out.

CLARK: Except Jack Archer. Skin smooth just like a baby's butt. Lucky creep.

DAVID: Some people luck out. What can I say?

CLARK: You think zits are world-wide thing?

DAVID: Sure. There are fast food dumps all over hell. They're busy dishing up greaseballs all over the globe.

CLARK: It's puberty. A lot of guys think it comes from whacking off.

DAVID: Naw. If that was the case, my face would disappear.

CLARK: Most guys get 'em. My dad had 'em.

DAVID: Mine too. Of course they had everything to hear them tell it.

CLARK: But worse, always worse.

DAVID: *(Noting his face.)* Jeez! Get a load of this one. A headlight.

CLARK: *(Noting the zit.)* Wow! You could get into Guinness with that one. The zit that ate Cleveland.

DAVID: Do you think pinching helps?

CLARK: What else can you do? If you don't, they grow up to be The Alps.

DAVID: Have you ever tried Oxy Clean Pads?

CLARK: I've tried everything. A dermatologist, even.

DAVID: I didn't know that.

CLARK: His complexion was worse than mine. It was like he washed his face with Liquid Plumber.

DAVID: If it weren't for Erase I couldn't leave the house. Like I'd just stay home and become like this weird teenage hermit, or something, you know? Zits, shit! Zits are a bitch.

DAVID: Yeah. Well, we can't just sit around on our butts worrying about it all the time. That would really be absurd, okay? Besides, you and I both know we'd go bananas for sure without women. It's not normal to not to want girls, okay? Hey, c'mon, let's get the hell outta here; this conversation is bumming me out.

CLARK: Yeah. We can't dwell on it, I guess.

DAVID: Right. So Let's go on down to the Dairy Store and suck up a couple a hot fudges?

I have eyes like those of a dead pig. Marlon Brando.

LES & JIM

The fellows discuss the rigors of their warehouse job.

LES: It's too much. Too much.

JIM: *(Slumping to a box, mopping his brow.)* Like *way* too much. Whew!

LES: Haven't these numbnuts ever heard of air conditioning?

JIM: They're too cheap for AC.

LES: Whew! It's a hot mother.

JIM: And some people actually like working.

LES: Can you believe it. Working's a crock. And how 'bout the idea of working fifty weeks and getting two weeks off?

JIM: I'd like to get my hands on the guy who thought that one up.

LES: And how 'bout that Earl?

JIM: Whatta dork.

LES: He actually likes this job.

JIM: He gets off on it. Like I said, Dork.

LES: He gets this glazed look in his eyes when he talks about how fast he can unload a truck full of refrigerators.

JIM: I know. And he digs the living shit out of assembling unfinished furniture. He holds some kind of record for throwing together a vanity table in ten minutes, or something.

(Pause as they sit looking about them.)

LES: Whew! Damn, it's hot.

JIM: *(Holding up his hand.)* Have you seen my thumb?

LES: *(Noting the thumb with horror.)* Wow. What happened?

JIM: I smashed it between a range and a wall downstairs.

LES: That's it, I've had it! I'm telling 'em to take this job and shove it sideways. Today.

JIM: You're kidding?

LES: Like hell. Hey! you call this a career, man? This here is insane, that's what this here is. Getting beat up, working like horses. And have you seen what rolled into the dock just before lunch?

JIM: Huh uh.

LES: A semi full of wallboard.

JIM: Wallboard?

LES: This humongus goddamned semi full of it. Forget it. I'm not about to go unloading that stuff. No way.

JIM: You're right, we quit. Who needs this? Do you realize what we'll wind up with if we unload that crap? Hernias, man, hernias. I'm quitting, too, even though my folks'll freak.

LES: So, they freak. So what? We're gonna risk hernias at our age for some stupid job?

JIM: I'm outta here.

LES: It's not like there aren't other after-school jobs.

JIM: Jobs where you don't have to bust your buns for short money and risk heat stroke and back problems and getting busted up. This place is the worst, the pits. Hey, like I wasn't cut out for ape work.

LES: *(Displaying his hands.)* Just get a load of my hands. Is this something? Is this a mess, or what?

JIM: *(Noting his own hands.)* Like mine. Like raw meat.

LES: So, we're outta here. We give 'em notice today, okay?

JIM: Plus the finger.

LES: All-right! Man, I just can't wait to see the look on their faces when we tell 'em to shove the wallboard.

JIM: Maybe the boss' old lady'll unload it. She's bigger and stronger than any of us.

LES: Yeah, and no risk of hernia.

JIM: Let's hit it. I'm dying in here. The next job we get they gotta have AC.

LES: Right.

JIM: I mean, hey, like kids have got rights, too, ya know?

LES: I understand the Velvet Dairy's looking for guys to work in their ice cream room.

JIM: Hey! You know it has to be cool in there.

LES: Right. Plus you probably get free fudgesicles and stuff.

JIM: Let's check it out.

    (As they exit, they flip the bird to the place.)

DONNY & FRED

Donny attempts to dissuade his friend from his deepening involvement with drugs.

DONNY: You gotta give it up.

FRED: Get lost!

DONNY: Dump it.

FRED: Go away.

DONNY: You're crazy.

FRED: Screw off!

DONNY: You gotta drop it, man. Just look at you.

FRED: I don't need the bullshit, okay?

DONNY: You're screwing up, man, screwing up bad.

FRED: Take a walk.

DONNY: Screwing up just like I did.

FRED: Yeah, right. So, don't come 'round pushin' advice on other people, okay?

DONNY: You're not "other people," man, you're my friend.

FRED: Alluva sudden like you get clean and now you're gonna go 'round layin' heavy duty shit on people because like you're better than them.

DONNY: You got it wrong.

FRED: Just lemme alone.

DONNY: You crazy hardheaded bastard. Look at you. You look like hell.

FRED: *(He seizes Donny by his shirt front.)* Hey! I ain't too loaded to kick butt!

DONNY: *(Shoving him away easily, violently.)* Don't wrinkle the shirt, crack-head!

FRED: Okay, okay!

DONNY: I want, I could flatten your ass. Because you've got nothing anymore. No muscle, no nothing. Look at you. You make me sick! *(Slaps Fred's face.)*

FRED: Hey!

DONNY: *(He slaps him again.)* Sick, I said. Sick!

FRED: Big man! Big man! Hey, I'd rather be bombed any day than be like you are straight! Like some preacher comin' 'round blowin' smoke an' mistreating 'is friends.

DONNY: You think this is neat, don't you, what you're doing to yourself? Messing yourself up like this, hurting your family, running yourself into the ground? Cute. Real cute. About as cute as cancer, that's what. Dumb ass. You make me sick.

FRED: *(Mocking.)* "You make me sick, you make me sick!" If I make you so sick how come you're coming 'round, huh, how come?

DONNY: Because I care about ya, you jerk, that's why; 'cause we've been pals since grade school; 'cause you're a cool guy who's messed up and because I know what you're going through because I've been there. Hey, man, you're a friend and like I worry about you, okay? *(He takes Fred by the shoulders.)* Understand? *(He shakes Fred gently.)* Don't you see what's happening to you, man? Don't ya? Freddy — you're killin' yourself. And it's killin' me to see it. Understand? Understand?

FRED: *(Collapsing into Donny's arms.)* Help me, man, help me.

BOY/GIRL

Impressions of Hollywood

The people are unreal. The flowers are unreal, they don't even smell. The fruit is unreal, it doesn't taste of anything. The whole place is a glaring, gaudy, nightmarish set, built up in the desert.— Ethel Barrymore.

The most important deals in the movie industry are finalized on the sun-drenched turf of golf courses or around turquoise swimming pools, where the smell of barbecue sauce is borne on gentle breezes and wafts over the stereo system of houses that people seldom leave.— Shirley Maclaine.

A place where they pay you $50,000 for a kiss and .50¢ for your soul.— Marilyn Monroe.

The only way to be a success in Hollywood is to be as obnoxious as the next guy. —Sylvester Stallone.

Hollywood provided the kind of luxury that exists today only for the sons of Latin-American dictators.—Groucho Marx.

A cultural boneyard.—Marlon Brando.

You can't find true affection in Hollywood because everyone does the fake affection so well.—Carrie Fisher.

DOUG & DORIS

They debate the older films vis-a-vis the more current offerings.

DORIS: Like take in "The Hucksters" when Sidney Greenstreet spits on the table and Gable reacts and right away you know that Gable isn't going to take any crap.
DOUG: So what?
DORIS: So Gable tells you all you have to know by this subtle little reaction. Like with a thing in his eyes.
DOUG: It was a stupid flick.
DORIS: "The Hucksters?"
DOUG: Most of those old films suck. Like "Gone With the Wind." The worst. My mom's all-time favorite. And they talk about the violence in today's pictures. Hey! Here you've got the Civil War in blazing color and in one scene this whole town's on fire and people are running around screaming and there's blood and bodies all over hell.
DORIS: That's nothing compared to the stupid "Friday the Thirteenth" stuff.
DOUG: Worse. Because it was more surrealistic; violence contrived in this kind of abstract way which gave it a more lasting impact.
DORIS: It was a great film. And great acting.
DOUG: It was awful. And the acting? Wow! Talk about sappy. Like the scene where Vivian Leigh's up on this phony back-lit hill screaming and doing this phony dramatic number. Terrible. We've got sluts in our drama class who can do better than that.

And what about that Butterfly-what's-'er-name person —
DORIS: McQueen.
DOUG: — running around like a chicken with it's head off with this voice like breaking glass. Do me a favor.
DORIS. A classic. Great. All of it.
DOUG: "Bat Man," now there's a picture. The idea, the effects, all of it.
DORIS: Boy, are you ever out of it. Comparing a piece of crap like that to "Gone With the Wind." It was lame. A stupid movie with overworked effects and Michael Keaton. This is a screen hero? The guy's got all the presence of an oyster. And then this phony car he drove looking like a hopped-up Pinto. A poop movie.
DOUG: You're locked in the past —
DORIS: Good.
DOUG: — with all that overacting and those sappy stories.
DORIS: They had human values. Like the Frank Capra stuff. Like, "It's A Wonderful Life."
DOUG: A piece of cornball junk.
DORIS: But you have to admit, Jimmy Stewart was great.
DOUG: James.
DORIS: Huh?
DOUG: Then James, now Jimmy. When he was a young guy he was James. Then, when he got old, it was Jimmy. Figure that out for logic. Twisted.

Like most of those stupid old flicks with silly stories and hammy acting.

DORIS: No way.

DOUG: Face facts.

DORIS: The older pictures were honest.

DOUG: They were corny.

DORIS: They were happening.

DOUG: They were naive.

DORIS: What about the Marx Brothers?

DOUG: What about them?

DORIS: They were the funniest.

DOUG: We've got just as funny today.

DORIS: Name one.

DOUG: Plenty.

DORIS: Name one.

DOUG: Plenty.

DORIS: Name one, airhead.

DOUG: Robin Williams.

DORIS: I may puke. You're comparing Robin Williams to the Marx Brothers?

DOUG: No. There were three of them and there's only one of him.

DORIS: I can't talk to you, you're out of it.

DOUG: And you're living in the past.

DORIS: At least it's living.

DOUG: I'm outta here. Let me know when you're ready to get real. *(He exits.)*

DINO & SUSAN

The subject is the suicide of a fellow classmate.

DINO: Did you hear about Chris Martinez?

SUSAN: No. What about him?

DINO: He shot himself.

SUSAN: He what?

DINO: He shot himself.

SUSAN: No!

DINO: I swear. Last Friday.

SUSAN: Wow.

DINO: He went home, went up to his room and shot himself. Just like that.

SUSAN: I just saw him last Thursday. He looked great, like always. Acted normal.

DINO: I know, that's what's so bizarre.

SUSAN: He wasn't the kind of person you would figure for problems, you know?

DINO: I guess you can never really tell about a person.

SUSAN: Chris, of all people. I mean, like an honor student, varsity football....

DINO: He was a cool dude.

SUSAN: Nothing ever seemed to get to him.

DINO: Yeah.

SUSAN: I never saw him when he wasn't happy. Maybe too happy.

DINO: How can you be too happy?

SUSAN: Nobody can be in a good mood all of the time.

DINO: Yeah. I guess everybody gets down once in awhile.

SUSAN: All that happy stuff must have been a cover up for being really unhappy. Can you imagine what he had going on inside?

DINO: I wonder why didn't he say something?

SUSAN: I don't know. He couldn't, I guess. Maybe he was too embarrassed, too afraid.

DINO: Afraid of what?

SUSAN: Of letting anybody know how he really felt. Like all of us sometimes.

DINO: Not me.

SUSAN: C'mon. You never cover up what you feel inside?

DINO: Well — ?

SUSAN: We all do. It's normal. But with guys like Chris I think it gets out of hand and they become depressed and stuff. You know?

DINO: I guess you're right —

SUSAN: Sure.

DINO: — about not letting stuff show, I mean. Like sometimes when I'm real down I crack a lot of jokes and stuff. Like I've got to be happier when I've got problems, when I'm depressed. You know?

SUSAN: But you come out of it.

DINO: Aw yeah, sure, sure, no problem.

SUSAN: That's normal.

DINO: Chris had this thing about always getting As in everything and being the best at sports and everything he did — everything. One time I saw him go ape and bust up a towel dispenser in the john

45

because he got a B. He must a been under some kind of pressure. Poor dude.

SUSAN: This makes the third kid this year.

DINO: Yeah: Bobby Sharp, Andy Diaz — and now Chris.

SUSAN: Sad, really sad.

DINO: If they'd just been able to talk, you know, to open up.

SUSAN: I guess they just didn't think they were good enough to be listened to.

DINO: Yeah.

SUSAN: And that's *really* sad.

Actors often behave like children and so we're taken for children. I want to be grown-up. Jeremy Irons.

MARCIE & CURT

Here a brother and sister discuss their futures. Curt intends to uphold family tradition, Marcie break the pattern.

CURT: Mom and Dad are really going to freak.
MARCIE: So, they freak.
CURT: It's like a family tradition.
MARCIE: Right. The boys go to Yale and the girls go to Smith. Big deal.
CURT: It's just the way it's always been, that's all.
MARCIE: A poor reason to screw up your life.
CURT: What'll it hurt? And it'll make them happy.
MARCIE: What about *my* happiness? What about me being just me instead of part of some stupid tradition? The whole Smith thing really turns me off. Besides, I'm not smart enough for Smith, anyhow.
CURT: Bull.
MARCIE: Not in this serious, intellectual way, I mean. I'm not bookish. Like mother was and grandmother. And, besides, being educated just to be educated isn't my thing.
CURT: Well, I'm really looking forward to Yale.
MARCIE: Sure. You've got Eli written all over you.
CURT: I also feel I have an obligation.
MARCIE: Obligation? Please — I may get sick on your bedspread. You're overwhelming sense of duty is nauseating.

CURT: Give me a damn break, okay? It's got nothing to do with duty. Look at it as being respectful.

MARCIE: It's duty—

CURT: No way.

MARCIE: — ten generations of ingrained attitude.

CURT: Call it what you want. Duty, whatever. It still makes sense.

MARCIE: Look at me, Curt. Do I really look like Smith material? C'mon now, be honest. Do I?

CURT: All the girls up there aren't serious intellectuals, okay? Bunny Rodgers sure isn't.

MARCIE: Bunny Rodgers gets As in everything. She's this living encyclopedia who's got a thing for Spinoza. And that's another thing — "Bunny." Her name says it all. "Bunny, Peetie, Binkie." I'd go ape surrounded by Bunnies and Peeties and Binkies for four years. All that preppy attitude and mentality. You come out of a school like that looking like a pair of penny loafers.

CURT: Where will you go?

MARCIE: Oh, I dunno, probably some nice little junior college somewhere. Where I can take courses in marketing and business.

CURT: Since when are you interested in business? This is the first I've heard of it.

MARCIE: I'd like to take a crack at retail.

CURT: You? In retail? You're putting me on?

MARCIE: It appeals to me.

CURT: We had some insanity back in the family, you know? I think it's finally starting to surface. Retail.

MARCIE: It's not a four letter word, you know.

CURT: I know, but —

MARCIE: There are a whole bunch of people out there selling and merchandising in case you weren't aware of it. Boy, are you ever sheltered.

CURT: What I mean is, it's way beneath you. You've got all this potential.

MARCIE: Who says? Mom and Dad say so because that's what they want to believe. Fact is — I'm an average student with average intelligence.

CURT: Smith would change that.

MARCIE: You talk like a person's doomed if he doesn't go to some heavy duty school.

CURT: Why sell yourself short?

MARCIE: I'm not. I'm just going to do what I want, that's all. I think it's something called freedom of choice.

CURT: Well, I'm going to Yale.

MARCIE: Was there ever any question? Hey, it's you. You're a Yale Man if there ever was one. Sure you'll go. And you should. You'll love it. Go for it. Stock up on blazers and striped ties and tweed caps and button-downs and have a blast. But me? Look for me at J. C. Penny.

LANA & ROD

Lana has just returned from "The Coast" and she's too hip. In this scene, Rod admonishes her for her super-cool attitude, affected mannerisms and speech.

(They meet.)

ROD: Lana! What's with the outfit? And the weird hair?

LANA: *(Displaying her wild mane proudly.)* You dig the cut?

ROD: No, I don't "dig" the cut. It's awful.

LANA: The hair's happening, man, happening.

ROD: And what's the deal with the talk?

LANA: Like what's with what talk like? What?

ROD: You know, the "happening" and "dig" and that.

LANA: Hey, I'm like just talking, man.

ROD: It's not "man." It's Rod, remember?

LANA: Yeah, man.

ROD: Jeez.

LANA: It's like how everyone talks on the coast. You knew I was out there, didn't you?

ROD: You're *out* there, all right.

LANA: I went out because Tom's there. He's doing gigs with this megaband.

ROD: Gigs with this megaband?

LANA: Like heavy metal, man. Five tons of blazing steel, babe. Wow, are they ever hot. You should dig 'em, they're super-rock. And they're up for this major deal with Capitol Records. This heavy-weight dude from the company fell by the club where they were wailing and really got off on their jams.

ROD: Lana, have you taken time out lately to give a good listen to yourself.

LANA: Why should I?

ROD: You're talking like a spaced out goon.

LANA: I am not!

ROD: Okay okay, forget it.

LANA: Like I was saying, this dynamite producer from Capitol thinks they're really smokin'. Like they're talking contract, man. Contract! You know what that means, don't you?

ROD: No.

LANA: Elephant dollars!

ROD: Elephant dollars?

LANA: Billboard bucks, man. Like the group's right now at this trashy club in the valley like where a lot of big acts got started. They're like ace, man, incredible, phenomenal, dy-no-mite!

ROD: Yes, but are they any good?

LANA: Heavy, like I said — heavy. Eric Clapton sat in with 'em one night and he was burnin', steamin', smokin'. Like I'm splitting back out next month. I gotta get my buns back there. I can't take any chances with a buff dude like Tom all alone out there with all those tight little units.

ROD: Lana, you've really lost it. All this phony talk and the hair and everything.

LANA: *(Running her fingers through her hair.)* You dig the orange streak?

ROD: *(Resigned.)* Yeah, it's very heavy.

LANA: I think so, too. Anyway, I'm splitting back because I really love Tom. Love 'im to the quantum. He's an ace dude. And he's gonna make it big. He's definitely a double platinum cat. I'm splitting just as soon's I get some bucks. I'm short right now but I'll get some dough or get Chinese-eyed trying. Besides, Tom really digs having me on the scene. Says I really amp him. He lives in this big pad in Venice. It's cool, fully munga.

ROD: Yeah, right, I totally dig. Like I'm solid behind your vibes, Lana. Like even though splitting to the coast is rad and you're still a squid you're old enough to know what you want and even though your parents'll freak you can't stay around here and veg out in this nothing burg because it would zap your mind because it's totally sixties. Like right, babe?

LANA: Rod?

ROD: Yeah?

LANA: Quit talking stupid.

I've always had the ability to say to the audience, watch this if you like, and if you don't, take a hike.
Clint Eastwood.

SANDY & BILL

Sandy blames the past for her problems instead of resolving old conflicts and moving on to healthy relationships.

SANDY: All of my life people have been telling me what to do. My mom, my dad, my teachers—everybody.

BILL: Maybe they know something you don't. Like how you're goofing up with this older guy.

SANDY: He's not old.

BILL: He's twice your age.

SANDY: So? So what?

BILL: You really think this guy cares about you? To him you're just another young slut.

SANDY: You don't know that!

BILL: Another young slut he can make it with and brag about to his friends. It's an ego thing. Another thing — the guys dealing drugs.

SANDY: So, so he has money. He's not some high school kid who works part-time at McDonald's.

BILL: I may work at McDonald's but I don"t have to look over my shoulder every time I leave the house. Face it, he's a scum-bag who uses the drugs to make it with young girls and get them involved. If you know what's good for you, you'll get out now.

SANDY: Don't give me advice, okay? I've had advice from my folks up to here, okay?

BILL: That's because they love you.

SANDY: Since when?

BILL: Since always.

SANDY: Then how come they never tell me? I never ever hear the words. Ever. It's like it would kill them if they said them; like they're poison in their mouth, or something.

BILL: Love doesn't always come out in words. It comes in understanding; it comes in feelings; in comes in carrying, Sandy.

SANDY: I've never felt wanted. It's like I'm this wind and I blow right past them and they can't see me, or something. It's like I'm not even here.

BILL: How could anyone not see a person like you?

SANDY: It's like I'm something that they can't relate to. I've always felt like this. Since I was a kid even. My sister and brother always got all the goodies. Me? nothing. You know what I do when I get home after school? I go right to my room because I don't feel like I'm part of anything.

BILL: *(Takes her by the shoulders.)* Hey, Sandy, listen to me here, okay? *(Pause.)* To me you're not the wind. To me you're really a neat person and someone special who I care about a lot and don't wanna see get wasted and flushed down the drain like so much garbage.

SANDY: Really? You really feel like that?

BILL: Look, I know like I'm not you're super zillionaire, or anything, but I think I can give you something this grease-ball never will — me.

SANDY: You?

BILL: Yeah. No drugs, no big time money deal — just me. And maybe, maybe every now and then I'll be able to sneak you a free Big Mac and fries.

DIALECT MONOLOGUES

by
Roger Karshner and David Alan Stern

13 ESSENTIAL DIALECTS APPLIED TO CONTEMPORARY MONOLOGUES.

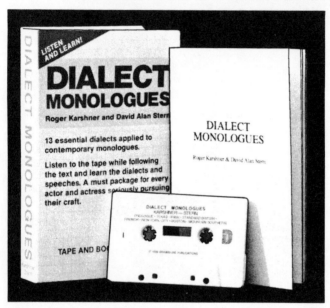

Book & Tape
$19.95

ISBN 0-940669-13-7

YOU LISTEN TO THE TAPE WHILE FOLLOWING THE TEXT AND LEARN THE DIALECTS AND SPEECHES. A MUST PACKAGE FOR EVERY ACTOR AND ACTRESS SERIOUSLY PURSUING THEIR CRAFT.

Here, for the first time, on **cassette tape** with a **corresponding book of monologues**, in one convenient package — **13 essential dialects**: TEXAS, IRISH, BRITISH, FRENCH, NEW YORK CITY, BOSTON, MOUNTAIN SOUTHERN, CHICAGO, GERMAN, YIDDISH, SPANISH, COCKNEY, and ITALIAN. And each has been applied to a **contemporary speech** (speeches which may be delivered — with or without the accent — for audition, workshop, and class room purposes).

The readings and instructional text are by Dr. David Alan Stern, dialectician to the stars — LYNN REDGRAVE, MIKE FARRELL, JACK KLUGMAN, EDWARD JAMES OLMOS, MICHAEL YORK, Oscar Winners OLYMPIA DUKAKIS, GEENA DAVIS, and many others.

The accompanying book of contemporary speeches is by Roger Karshner whose outstanding Dramaline publications are widely recognized by amateurs and professionals.

AN INNOVATIVE, INVALUABLE TOOL FOR EVERY ACTOR.

DRAMALINE PUBLICATIONS

ORDER DIRECT